JUDIT

PLEASURE SEEK

his volume intr
oughton Mifflin New
esigned to bring atter
g new poets an
oughton Mifflin's
st of distinguished
A thoughtful and
aster, Judith Lee
nguage, an atmo
d rhythm all h
easure Seeker's
ver a univers
rangeness, capt
d remoteness.
deterministic wo
ed feelings bi
ons. The po
rongly philoso
icting charact
assions in oth
respond. As
ted poetic por
dith Leet bri
strivers wl
cious, al
is fir

continued from front flap

ences the longer works of W. H. Auden and Chaucer, but brings to bear upon her work a new and unique sensibility that pits a clear-eyed vision against a world of mad circumstance.

JUDITH LEET, who attended Radcliffe College and the Pennsylvania Academy of Fine Arts, has been writing for a number of years and has published work in literary periodicals. She works full time as a free-lance editor and writer for scientific publications, is a devoted amateur musician, and has published illustrations in national magazines. Judith Leet lives in Chestnut Hill, Massachusetts, with her husband, Professor Kenneth Leet, and their son and daughter.

PLEASURE SEEKER'S GUIDE

◆ Houghton Mifflin New Poetry
Pleasure Seeker's Guide by Judith Leet

Judith Leet

PLEASURE
SEEKER'S
GUIDE

Houghton Mifflin Company
Boston : 1976

Library of Congress Cataloging in Publication Data

Leet, Judith.
Pleasure seeker's guide.

(Houghton Mifflin new poetry)
I. Title.
PS3562.E373P5   811'.5'4   75-45200
ISBN 0-395-24313-0
ISBN 0-395-24347-5 pbk.

Printed in the United States of America

W   10   9   8   7   6   5   4   3   2   1

To E. H. and H. H.

> . . . whatever comes
> One hour was sunlit and the most high gods
> May not make boast of any better thing
> Than to have watched that hour as it passed.

— Ezra Pound

CONTENTS

5. Compensations

PART I
The Given

OVERLOOKING THE PILE
OF BODIES AT ONE'S FEET

Is it a victory of sorts
not to be discouraged
if everything goes badly
for over twenty years?

Or should one be discouraged
and how much?

All the good I've tried to do
that didn't work out
through my own fault
and the fault of others.

You never know much conclusively.
Not able to know the truth,
pick the "expedient form of error,"
Vaihinger advises
in *Die Philosophie des Als-Ob,*
last chapter.

    1.

Openly telling Evan Haven
of my shift in feelings —
despite admitting that I liked him
for a year, perhaps two,

and letting him care for me
as much as he liked;
nevertheless, I had the right
to withdraw my affection —

he didn't need to change jobs,
night schools, rooms, cities,
drive five thousand miles away
from me. He was an extremist
who subscribed to extreme positions.

It was up to him to know
whether I am worth running from or dying for,
whether I am an ass or not or worse.
(Should I say ass about myself or let others?
E. Brontë used ass in print with authority —
"Have you found Heathcliff, you ass" — in her time.)

Evan crushed himself inside his car —
a black Buick with red trim —
against the circular end
of a Sun Oil truck.

I myself assumed
he was reading Kant while driving,
an execrable habit of his;
he did not live to complete
the philosophy degree.

His brother thought that Evan,
missing me, had made the decision
to die and took any opportunity
that offered him oblivion.

2.

Should I have left him less abruptly?
One winter afternoon, with no preparation,
I told him I was moving that evening —
to look for someone of fewer moods.

All my questionable acts and evil works —
both those I have done unwittingly
and those I know about —
I have justified to my own satisfaction:

as a practising determinist,
I feel that all my actions
are without exception predetermined;
whatever I chose to do in the past
was the single choice available to me —

the unavoidable consequence
of my earlier mistreatment by others.
Years of exposure to the influence
of small-minded, ungenerous humans
make me respond as I do.

One's sense of choice
persists as an illusion.

3.

Then some five years later,
another close friend, Edward Edgeworth,
drove a used blue Ford —
a metallic acid shade of blue
I didn't care for —

through a concrete guard wall,
through a protective wire network,
and out over the ominous
icy Mystic River far below,
diving in his car.

Short of time to effect a rescue,
the police gaffed him with an ugly spike
and bruised him further —
but he was already obliviously dead

from drowning and from blood loss
of severe cuts and gashes,
and all his teeth and fingers
were missing in the water.

Why did they try to revive him
in such an unenviable condition?

He left a note, not too self-pitying,
both taped and nailed to my door:
that he wanted to be buried
inside his car was his last wish,

the used blue Ford, also rescued
by police. The authorities
on the Burial Committee refused;
the clergy equivocated
and deferred to the committee.

4.

One's usual bureaucratic reaction:
the institution before the individual need;

that it was unprecedented;
that it might initiate a trend

of mechanical devices, wheelchairs, rowboats,
for which they would be pressed for space.
Hard enough to fit all the qualified bodies —
already, for strangers, unseemly close.

O GOD. Wearied by that type
of rule for rule's sake mind,
I actively encouraged my friends
to be buried at sea.

Unforgivable lack of respect
for a last wish. An inviolable request
of the dead, now beyond helping himself.
That Edgeworth might never know
was my only consolation —
after trying all the burial plots
of various churches.

    5.

Once more I needed to explain
my harmful influence on others,
which I did after making certain changes
in my relationship to a personal God.

I had taken up a faith provisionally
after Evan's death — to temper
my strict determinism
with a warm, if imaginary, Advisor.

Where was the all-knowing guidance
that I would require in a god?

He should not allow me into
such confusion without more help.
At this point, I abandoned Him.

6.

Edward Edgeworth left a second note
that he mailed before he died
saying "try not to blame yourself too much,"

but that I drove him directly to it
to prove the completeness of his love,
believing that the sacrifice
of his life and self and all he was
was the only irrefutable proof of his love.

Should I have felt worse than I did?
He was the one at fault;
he was the destructive one
diving his car from the bridge

the day after I told him —
with carefully constructed, gentle phrases,
remembering Evan's extremist reaction —
that I did not suit his needs.

His final words were
he hoped I would miss him.
Double damn fart if I would.
I kicked in a rented door
for which I was subsequently forced to pay.

However, should I be touched
that he wanted to die for me —
or rather for lack of me? It's a great honor
from a certain point of view.

I myself would never dive off a bridge
for him — or anyone.
No one is worth it, in my opinion.

7.

"I have never received
the necessary cooperation,"
another young friend, Victor Cloud,
confided just before his suicide.

For at least three days he writhed
from the bed to the floor to the bed.
And on several occasions he changed
his mind in favor of living.

I would prowl through the hospital
at night to ferret out the doctor —
who would hide from me
if he saw me in time to hide —
with a revised message from the patient:

"At the moment he wants to live" or
"Right now he prefers you allow him to die" —
whatever our most recent thought.

While we waited for the antidotes to work
or not, I helped Victor to consider
whether he truly cared to live on,
or persist with his suicide attempts,

or try a month's more life —
if he lived, that is —
and suicide after that, if practicable.

8.

Endless complications to the question
of Victor's living or not,
which the doctor refused to go into.
He sided entirely with life —
regardless of its meager prospects.

Sarah, Victor's wife of a month,
had left him for his closest friend, Omar.
His first book was reviewed as
"worthless, unreliable, and best withdrawn"
by this same ubiquitous, slippery Omar.

Victor's next four books were never completed:
he had grown too much the perfectionist
to call any work of his resolved. Penultimately
Victor was asked to leave the classics
department by its new head, Omar.

That I didn't want him with me
permanently — now highly distraught —
was the final addition
to his cumulative despair.

At times he was more living than dead,
more green and black than white; lying in vomit,
he always missed the receptacle provided.
I held his head into the pain.

9.

Three days of his dying
was the next step,

lasting three months.
The imposition on my time
was one of my responses.

My inner clocks, the world's clocks,
slowed to a church service.
I could not expunge these hours.
Whenever I checked the time,
the clock over the nurse's head,
it was five in the morning, five, five.

Victor wanted me to stay by him
at all times, not to let him die
unheld in human arms, slip off
alone in a room unnoticed,
without his last words heard.

I thought he asked too much,
but as his only friend on hand,
probably his only friend on earth —
he had insulted all the others —
I prowled the corridors
and begged myself not to desert him.

Christ, how could I help,
afraid as anyone comes?
But I reassured him, hoping to provide
for his need, whatever it was,
by comforting words: "At least death
brings release from one's fears of dying."

Conscious of the last wish
as, for me, sacred and inviolate —
I remembered Edgeworth's love of his Ford,

how defiantly I had slipped the steering wheel
in with him, as a temporizing measure —
I promised Victor I would see him through his death.

10.

They pumped and aspirated Victor.
Oxygenated and transfused him.
Catheter. Three IV's in his arms.
Tracheotomy. Respirator.

His vital signs were flagging.
The medical teams would not admit it
but they were giving up.
Victor Cloud died one sunny morning —
unhappily in one of his living moods.

All theories have their weaknesses:
I have now rejected determinism.
Although it explains my past actions —
that I was helpless to do other
than what I did and helpless to avoid
improper early influences —
it offers little guidance forward.
Presently adrift,
I am now seeking out
a more sustaining ideology.

Is it a victory of sorts
not to be discouraged
if everything goes badly
for over twenty years?

Or should one be justifiably
discouraged — and how much?

J. ROBERT'S
MENTAL APPARATUS

1.

I was seated on J. Robert's knee
unwinding a curl beguilingly,
using my smile for the spring on a trap,
deploying my eyes on campaigns

to suggest he want to hold me by a breast
to help me balance on his knee,
and hoped he would request that I
lay my clean curls on his silk tie.

J. Robert was a disciplined ascetic
in the field of quantum physics;
his unforgetting enemies were everyone
whose mistakes of theory he refuted
by his insertions of pellucid logic.

Born world-weary, *fin de siècle* as a child,
he deplored the role of body —
the time to tend, to dress, to feed it;
he consented to the role of mind —
monkish, spartan, the thinnest of thinkers.

A contempt of lesser minds
cost him everyone but me:
I would give him my mind as a weakness
but I hoped my wit would hold him.

Eyes half-raised, half-shut,
in a torpor of fatigue from recent analyses —
he had overstressed his mental apparatus
and now waited languidly to recover.

2.

Two guards in counterspy disguise
were posted outside the door with twenty guns
to protect the valued mind in my lap
against assassins, spies, and any Russians.

Cleaning their weapons, playing Hearts,
hourly checking his head for signs of life,
the agents made lewd remarks on J. Robert's
potency, on the government using him for stud
to raise a crop of *wunderkinder*.

His head now shaded by my left breast,
we rested together on a white-washed balcony
overlooking yellow mimosas, a tropical grotto,
and sun-burnt water of a blinding blue.

I skimmed my past for its interest;
I pleaded with my mind for its wit.
I spoke of permanent and transient love,
how I favor the former; the other withers.

"Like a virgin undone, permanent love
is not found more than a single time, or
unlike a virgin undone, more than two
or three times. Transient love, however,
from the start implies decay."

Only his own numerical arrays and
speculations absorb J. Robert wholly.
What will hold him to me, as he removes himself,
while warm in my arms, to be with his mind?
And needs no one.

3.

As he lies in my lap, his head now shaded
by a silk awning — the guards fear sunstroke —
shall I tell him I draw, usually in ink,
and specialize in double profiles
of lovers, almost kissing,

their mouths hovering, but always apart,
suspended in space for tension.
The only art lover who asked to buy one —
a patron at last — died the next day,
before she had the chance. Sad for both of us.

Or shall I tell him of my other minor gift,
writing many starts of plays
but abandoning the hard, intractable parts —
the denouement, the ending, the characterization?
My ability to write with wit is limited,
but J. Robert might not conceive of a mental limitation.

Or shall I sing for him my repertoire
of *cante jondo,* gypsy lovelife songs,
those from deep in bed with a partner of spirit:
"No quiero decir, por hombre, las cosas que ella me dijo"
in my quavering, quasi-Spanish manner,

strumming the miniature zither
I keep always on a chain about my neck,
eyes shut, eyebrows knit in pain —
songs that suggest the hearer
find a passing lover and rush into trouble?

Or shall I say nothing of myself,
act the part of a mirror-enigma?
I compete for J. Robert's affection
and time against his own elitist mind.

4.

J. Robert should not be overpraised,
in my opinion, for working well within
a mental facility of such distinction;
given his capable mind from birth,
you or I might have achieved as much.

One hundred thousand formulas
he could interchange in his thoughts,
fitting complexity to complexity,
from all the theoretical areas of science.

His failing was an impatience
with the lack of intuition for theories
of quanta in his colleagues: he made known
his indifference to routine brilliance.

J. Robert created his future enemy-to-death
by pointing out — no, ridiculing —
errors of computation and logic
at a now infamous symposium.

5.

At noon we moved inside to his narrow cot
and now lie facing each other,
his silk tie slipped between us.
I am alone with Robert's body.
His mind might or might not be present.

I study his eyes, close up and closed;
his pink-gray eyelids shiver nearby.
Shaded by imaginary lemon trees,
I breathe the lemon of his skin.
Being together brings us no closer;
I deflect him
from the advancement of science.

6.

All too late I asked myself
did his mental apparatus come between us
or was it the hunchback mathematician
that lured him away, Miss Musetta Truitt,
a megacephalic, with a facile brain
and a sensitive face for a dwarf.

I'll have to console myself —
and wait for the wounds never to heal —
by singing "all is lost" songs from my repertoire
in an assumed, indifferent voice — beyond caring.

My self-deceptions do not help me:
often I forget to sing in an undaunted manner;
I notify myself I care, I care, and
will always care for J. Robert.

❖

Once despite our being on vacation
in early evening he set to work;
a swelling, a pressure of his crowded thoughts
had to be drawn off. At intervals
he soaked his forehead in a vase of ice.

The guards and I played Hearts,
more games in a row than I had ever played,
letting him think at the full reach of his powers,
until he found the inevitable logic.

We brought him black Kenya coffee, his favorite;
refusing it, he ordered green Lapsang tea.
We brewed the tea; he insisted he had said
a white wine. So abusive, so insulting was his manner
that one of the guards threatened to shoot him.

Even a mind like J. Robert's miscalculates.
After twenty hours of steady application,
he announced his answer of zero was wrong;
with his mind in ruins and unusable for days,
he spent the week resting his head on my lap
watching the water sunning in the grotto.

MISSILE LAUNCH OFFICER

To A. I. C. L.

"Although I felt too young for the responsibility,
I was waiting for a message from the president
to launch a nuclear attack against our enemies —
whoever they turned out to be.

"For four years I waited impatiently,
sixty feet underground in a buried chamber
placed on a steel plate suspended by four springs —
and carefully watched a board with blinking lights.

"My given task was to implement
what was known as the Total War Plan (TWP),
that is, to remove everyone from sight."
"Were you willing to remove everyone?" "That is secret."

"Please don't tell me anything
that I'm not allowed to know."
"I won't give you any secret information;
the problem is, instead, do you want to know?

"My standing orders were to decode the message
when it came, insert the key — and to press the button
with the objective certainty
of all great leaders and executioners.

PART II

Aspirations

A SUITABLE FIELD

To K. H. M. L.

1.

In music, dear lady, I began my career:
French horn and timpani both were my instruments.
I believed I wanted to work at my music full time, that
so roused, so moved by music, I must neglect all else.
But this becomes akin to what in time?
To kissing one's ladylove so steadily that
one loses one's interest, one's sport, one's zest,
and wants only a spartan, occasional kiss.

2.

I packed my instruments in fitted cases
(a trust on father's side, an ironworks,
paid my tuition bills from 1906)
and left forever the Budapest Conservatoire —
Liszt's old haunt — after ten years
of steady practice. I only later missed my power,
in timpani parts, to drown the others out
completely. If you had been fortunate enough
to hear my *Harold in Italy* — *subito fortissimo* —
I startled the hall. Hah! The audience thought
it had been shot in the back.

3.

Thereafter I pursued another of my interests—painting,
to add, Miss Parsh, to the world's supply of beauty.
I most admired a style no longer in style —
but which I hoped to revive — the early Flemish,
the so-called Netherlandish painter, Rogier van der Weyden,
a primitive to some but not, by God, to me.
His lack of fluency at his task appealed
to a tight strangling I felt in me — the constricted line
and acid greens and siccity expressed his struggle,
and mine, to speak without the native bent
of, say, a Rubens, noted for his facile brushing.

4.

Accompanied by horn and timpani, I hired a studio,
formerly Corot's, and entered an Ecole des Beaux-Arts
near Dijon. No one — I was informed too late —
had taught the primitive style since Le Douanier
Rousseau, my idol, had perished of critical abuse.
(His *Sleeping Gypsy* and *Jungle Dreams* improve
my life.) Set at once to drawing plaster casts
of Roman copies of lost Greek works — precisely
in the manner of academies to miss the point
of what one needs — I was taught in the classic,
not archaic style, to the lure of which I succumbed,
and dropped at once my former masters — Rogier,
Uccello, Gentile, and even Le Douanier — as untrained.

5.

My curious attempts to draw in charcoal
what appeared on the dusty casts — the presence

of layers of muscles throbbing under the skin —
were problematic to Gérard Gérôme, the drawing master,
who never had a student of my willingness.
In time I advanced to drawing the female nude:
I struggled into the studio, eyes to skylight
and back to wall — not to notice myself
in this compromising spot, circa 1910,
with no experience of undressed ladies
staring at me. I sensed my own disapproval.

6.

The shock of these disproportionate flaccid models —
in the crabbed, pinched style of Lucas Cranach —
upon my sensitivity to form, the gap between
the former ideal of the casts and the present state of flesh —
I missed my Greeks, their flow, their level of success.

7.

After eight years of studio work, I learned
to mix and apply the paint with assurance;
I studied glazes, stretchers, rabbits' skin glue,
the uses of stand oil, poppy oil,
and sun-thickened linseed oil,
lead white, flake white, zinc white,
the other hues, varnishes, and fugitive shades.
Indeed I was equipped for a career as an artist
when I recognized I had no necessary subject:
I had no face, no form, no shape, no shadow
that an inner imperative moved me to paint.
O God, what a dismal error, a quagmire.
How could I explain this to myself and others?

8.

Having completed three large outdoor scenes of nudes,
a Roman campagna, a study of black and purple tulips,
a self-portrait with fingers lightly touching the frame,
and an Ecce Homo, I had wholly lost the need
to express *le beau* for the world's museums.
I had, as well, such criteria of taste
that I could never attain my minimal standards.

9.

During this crisis, I resumed my search
for a field to enlist my energies.
My contemporaries by now all knew their type
of work, their plan of life, but I did not —
as we all know — now forty-four,
the alarm of others partially justified.
Casmir — was he a friend or an alarmist? —
suggested a school of analysts in Wien
for my prolonged dissatisfactions. I felt, however,
my search for a suitable field could not justify
the time of a neurologist taken
from his more pressing cases.

10.

Encumbered by horn and timpani, plein air nudes,
tulip study, self-portrait, Ecce Homo (fairly large),
and learning more and more, if not precisely what
I was meant to do or was working toward,
I forced myself to Tübingen to continue my researches.

11.

No longer needing the undefined emotions of music,
no longer taken with the idol-making of art,
and feeling that my mind had been neglected,
a third direction — stemming from my indirection —
presented itself to me, concerning human knowledge:
how one knows, or if one can know with any certainty.
Or if one settles for illusions.
The notion that I was late, too late at forty-four
to undertake a whole new field, did not dissuade me.
I do wish you to understand quite well, Miss Parsh,
the conscious basis for all the actions taken.

12.

At first I thought to confront the systems of Kant
or Hegel — known to be complex (I welcomed the complexity) —
but German not being the native habit of my mind,
I moved from Tübingen to Edinburgh to study
David Hume, investigator of mental processes.
Absorbing his entire corpus, I became a devoted Humean,
a complete convert: theories of contingency, causation,
resemblance, and contiguity were welcome in my mind.
In *An Enquiry Concerning Human Understanding,*
Hume posited that the faculty of reason alone
isolated from experience was severely restricted:
that "the sun will not rise tomorrow" cannot be refuted
without one's having seen the opposite repeatedly.
And even seeing the sun rise every day —
as I interpret Hume — does not allow one's reason
to presume that it will rise again tomorrow.
It may well not. Envision a limited cosmic catastrophe —
say an unknown force diverting our sun. I fully agree

that "all laws of nature and all the operations of bodies,
without exception, are known only by experience."

13.

I now quote from Leszek Kolakowski
commenting on Hume: "What can be asserted
beyond doubt is limited to individual accounts
of immediate observations," which I take to mean:
I can only know for certain, without disquietude,
the single thought I have in mind just now —
assuming I have registered an accurate perception.

14.

I found much imprecision in the field of Hume studies,
much disagreement, in commentaries, on his intended meaning.
I felt my contribution would be to refute
all misinterpretations with complete and detailed
arguments — forcing all detractors into submission.
After ten years of effort, my mind overburdened,
I was too feeble to eat or dress or call for assistance,
and remained in bed, half-starved — I have been told —
reciting long passages from Hume.

15.

Now aided by the aforementioned Casmir —
who was pleased to see his earlier fear for my mind
prove true — I spent nine years in treatment with an analyst,
reluctantly storing my instruments and paintings,
voluminous notes and half-completed text on Hume.

16.

Dr. Holst agreed I had not yet found, despite true efforts,
a suitable field and advised me to proceed as before —
even if it took more years than one's allotted lifetime —
that the need or determination, in my case, to find my field
of endeavor must subordinate all extraneous considerations
of a calm mind or composed, routine well-being,
that I was one of those perverse individuals who would
not settle for facile attunement with the universe.

17.

Now in Salzburg, a rainy quiet spot for work,
reassured, almost elated, inwardly regrouped,
I settled in the center of a palatial room,
unpacked my books, spread out my papers,
reread my chapters on Hume (quite pleased
with the orderly exposition), and hung the Ecce Homo,
punctured in three places while in storage.

18.

I prepared to resume my researches at once;
I would now attempt to consolidate, at last,
essential concepts from my three disparate subjects —
in a possible synthesis. If I could adapt
the rhythms that support all musical structure,
the keen attention to image-making in art,
and the rigorous scrutiny of ideas from Hume,
I would attempt an interdisciplinary study:
"Toward an Understanding of Human Endeavors"
that might disperse all doubters, including myself,

and alleviate my embarrassment at being so unsettled
over such long stretches of my lifetime.

19.

Upon rumination, however, a further doubt emerged:
I should study — at least somewhat — the earth
or life sciences, particularly their numerical methods,
before I feel myself ready for the proposed synthesis —
in case I have missed an approach that would alter my results.
And have therefore sent for various catalogues
at the appropriate institutes of science and technology.

20.

With tulip study, timpani, French horn, books, and music stand,
the Ecce Homo, the Hume manuscript, a blue-tiled Salzburg
    stove,
with all this weighty accumulation, I shall press on —
possibly closer than ever to finding a suitable field.
At least Dr. Holst and I understand and approve
the nature of my actions, even if all others are mystified.

FULFILLMENT

Is it enough of an ambition
to want to have been Hector Berlioz?
Or that master sensualist, Johannes Brahms,
that bringer of longing, that mover of spirit?
But not able to be either of them —
they having already lived and written well —
is it enough of an ambition
to want to lie on a narrow sofa,
preferably undisturbed,
and hear their works played all afternoon
by adept musicians on my monophonic record player?
And allow the sounds to evoke in me
a passion I have never felt for anyone.

MEGAN'S PERCEPTIONS

(The Tutor's Pupil's Tale)

Among her admirers was a piano virtuoso
known for his Schumann interpretation.
A much-praised writer of the film *Olga and Osip*
begged for her attention, for an evening, a moment.
A young philanthropist was one of those she tired of
and left abruptly — at a party in his honor.
Indifferent to all, she refused their offers
impartially, without reviewing individual needs.

"My plans for the next two weeks are made by now.
In three or four weekends, I should be free;
you might call then. To be entirely truthful,
which is what I wish to be, my plans are made a year ahead
and are to have no plans — to leave the days quite free
expressly for working out the mood I'm in.
To be entirely truthful, I do not care to know you any better."
Many, undeterred by her precision, offered themselves again.

"To reciprocate the love of all my volunteers
is quite beyond my abilities — or wishes."
She felt the pressure of admirers had harmed her,
had turned her vicious to save herself.
Inured to suffering on her behalf, she acted blameless
and imposed upon. Among the admirers she mistreated
or cut down were various surgeons, a corporate banker,
a prince of Hesse-Darmstadt — any of whom I felt was worthy.

Allow me — or skip on — the effusions her appearance demanded.
Her moist, lush, lavish eyes — the black mirror in the center
circle was rimmed in vibrant cobalt blue. Her nostrils
were an intricate figure eight of narrow gauge.
Her lips were wide, smooth pads to cushion kisses;
her cheeks, reputedly the softest in existence — as soft
as sifted and resifted earth. Even I felt drawn to touch
her cheeks and test the softness. Her hair was a jumbled
cloud-like fleece in which one hoped to be mislaid.

The intellectual, Gustav Ringelbach, called from Zurich.
I was to pass the message that she did not care to speak.
He begged for her. No reason I suggested moved her
to the open wire from Zurich, that narrow tunnel of sound.
He threatened to shoot himself at once — while on the phone
for her to hear. Still, in the timeless pose
of Canova's *Venus Victrix*, she refused to act.
"You may listen to him shoot himself but I prefer to read."

On his birthday, the virtuoso called from Basel.
She refused to speak. He begged me to intervene.
I begged her. She resisted all our reasoning
for endless minutes. "In Basel," I pleaded, "with no one,
no pleasures, insensate from touring and recitals." At last
Megan held the phone at the far end of her outstretched arm
and said, "She is not in." "I do not hear you. Are you speaking,
Megan, is it you? I can never reach you. Who keeps you from
     me?"

"If it is difficult to reach me, it's due
to others — wholly not my fault. I'm engaged
much of the time in turning down invitations,
sorting requests, writing excuses and regrets —
forgetting I've accepted whom for which occasion —
deciding where I want to go and weighing the type

of time I'll have and if I want to have it. At present,
I go out much less: the unsorted thoughts of friends
are typically not worth hearing. I prefer to read —
more orderly thinking than one's routine conversations."

The virtuoso called once more from Milan to report
his triumphs: "the skills, the artistry displayed . . ."
She dropped the phone. It spiraled,
spiraled on its wire, wound and unwound,
his voice afloat in the room, translating from the Italian.
What present might he bring her?
"I cannot be bribed by anyone or you;
it gives the rich and fair unfair advantage."
She insulted him inhumanly — in her most insulting manner.

Abruptly Megan handed me the phone. "Goodnight,"
I said in her behalf, "and kind of you to call."
"The virtuoso is agreeable as virtuosos go," she observed,
"but our conversation on his success disinterests me.
Again I am distracted by others and neglect my studies.
My Greek is slipping; my German is weaker.
Without a greater effort, the speed at which I learn
my languages just equals that at which I lose them.
I have found a private tutor to force me to reform."

She vowed to rid herself of admirers more ruthlessly,
whom I pictured waiting in spiral lines on endless lawns.
"I take no interest in any of them; I see their weakness:
that they admire someone who is shallow and unformed.
How can I form a favorable opinion of another's judgment
who admires someone as shallow, unrealized, and incomplete
as I know myself to be? To be entirely truthful,
they pursue someone simply not worth having."

And I, still unknown to you, much-appreciated reader,
I was out of contention for her love
owing to my well-controlled desires and the insight
that I had no chance. With a flourishing moustache
behind which I hide and an atypical forehead that pitches
forward at my hairline, I was in the honored position
of advisor and helped her interpret the world as best we could:
although my advice was rarely accepted and more rarely
followed, she consulted me on all occasions.

◆

Mademoiselle Berthe, first Megan's tutor, then mine,
confided to me that Megan employed *"trop d'honnêteté,*
more honesty than anyone could bear,"
and missed the equipoise of an Ingresque beauty,
"par exemple Mademoiselle Rivière," since each of her features
was overblown *"seulement un peu"* for the classic canon.
But Berthe, whose features were both cramped and asymmetric,
might well have spoken in her own missing beauty's behalf.

Although her hitherto noted inability to love is
unexplainable even by me, the omniscient writer,
Megan informed me that, at last, she was attracted to
the conductor and former prodigy Roland LaPlace
at whose debut at ten the critics pronounced, "unready,"
and who, now at forty, awaited appointment to a major post.
His conversation dealt with technical details of tempi:
"The *allegro non troppo* in relation to my imagined
     perfection . . ."
With an air of savior to his art, he wearied me.

That Megan was unknown in any field, LaPlace contended —
with no natural gift, no area to enter
that would make her known to the cognoscenti,

with no body of work to show for her years alive —
was a grave defect in meeting his requirements
for a friend; he would consider only a scholar or specialist,
an Edith Sitwell, Caroline Spurgeon, Wanda Landowska,
Georgia O'Keeffe — one who had proved herself as set apart

by passion and single-purposedness in some field.
Or at least someone whose wealth was sufficient
to offset the lack of all this other.
Roland — who sported the single earring of a Don Giovanni,
knitted headgear, and a fur swaddling cape —
and I — who wore only unobtrusive clothes — were opposites.
I perceived him as a personal enemy and a solipsist;
that I know of, he expressed no interest
in forming an opinion of me.

"What will encourage Roland to love me?
All the others find me effortless to love.
Shall I study the Berlioz *Memoirs* — he recommended it —
the Mozart family correspondence, Schweitzer on Bach?
Take up musical analysis? Or composition?
Roland admires self-made minds, but — lacking discipline
and steadiness — I fall back on my unearned beauty
and its power. And we know he is oblivious to beauty."

After careful reflection on her reasonable chances,
I advised that she should try to love instead
one of all the others waiting outside in line.
I observed that none of my most pressing wishes
had ever come to pass as I had hoped;
I then had had no choice but to revise my wishes.
Insisting my advice was incorrect, she sent me out:
"Agree that Roland will come to find in me
the qualities the others find self-evident."

Doubting that Roland's indifference could be reversed,
still I hoped she might prevail — to spare herself all
the fasting, vigils, attempts at self-improvement,
and other methods so far ineffectual to mollify
the god in charge of those in her unloved position.
Reader, I confess that I understand no one's
mode of thinking — not yours, not mine — and understood
our Megan's least: I found LaPlace unworthy of her pain.

She sent him all-inclusive letters, no thought of hers
neglected, sent revisions and further revisions
of each letter, drawings of herself both clothed and nude
(commissioned from an artist friend of Berthe's, who copied
Bonnard's style), a plaster cast of her flawless fingers,
diary pages expressing her detailed response
to his most recent concert — the range, the type,
the shading of her emotions — and suggesting a capacity to feel
was her most engaging attribute.

Using methods I felt harmed her case,
she arranged to meet him, uninvited, after his rehearsals,
to foresee his appointments, to place herself where he might be.
Astounded at her luck, she rented an apartment with windows
facing his and took up a vigil, watching him
talk to himself, kiss the hands of imaginary patronesses,
practice his conducting gestures, and study his face
in a three-way mirror. He never drew his blinds
and lived in open view of her observatory.

After neglecting my advice — always to abandon Roland —
she sought and followed the advice of all:
experts on unrequited love, astrologists,
readers of palms, tea leaves, birthmarks;
she would follow the advice of waiters, bank tellers,

and passing vagrants. For the first three years,
she pursued him in a bold offensive, by attack and ambush.
For the second three years, she hoped to alter
his neural processes by electronic devices
and by transpersonal thought alignment.

In a typical effort, she borrowed a fuchsia gown,
circled her eyes with a violent outline,
practiced the release of her smile and a processional walk.
At Roland's final bow, with arms extended horizontally,
she descended the center aisle, catching two thousand eyes,
and bowed to the floor at his feet. "The effect worked out
as planned. The audience approved the gesture, everyone asking
who I was — except Roland who knew and disapproved."

❖

After six years of Megan's steady pursuit
(was he ever led to reconsider?), LaPlace married
unexpectedly one Micolette Rue, a harpsichordist,
expert on Scarlatti and his contemporaries, sole heiress
to the Rue Bridge and Rue Steel holdings,
owner of original Poussins and a rare Georges de La Tour,
enigmatic, virtually silent, revealing herself
only in her performance of Scarlatti.

Frenzied, Megan at first could not accept her sudden loss,
called Miss Rue adulteress and undistinguished (both untrue),
but shortly thereafter reversed herself — to acknowledge
the existence and unfairness of the marriage.
At a farewell dinner we two held to eulogize her loss
of LaPlace, she agreed to accept Micolette's ascendency —
and not merely as a temporary interlude. "That I lost him
in the disciplined effort of my life thus far proves
that I am capable of taking strong and continuous,
if in this case useless, action."

Upon release from this constrictive fixation,
Megan married one among her still-faithful — the architect
Wilbraham Loomis, who earned in time much praise
for his lucid structures and uncommon uses of space.
Designer of embassies, pavilions, villas, and residences,
he personally restored the private tower as a current taste.
Loomis, capable and stable if somewhat harassed
by clients' demands, was to me a more acceptable choice
in every respect than LaPlace. Their four children
were named Megan, Berthe, Wilbraham — and Roland.

"I introduced myself before a Sunday afternoon recital;
Micolette has many moles, bulging eyes, thin gray lips —
but we know that Roland is untouched by beauty or its absence.
She sat before a full-length mirror, dipping her fingers
in warm water, reviewing the scores; she feared a memory lapse.
Human of me, I wanted her to stumble more than once.
Having heard of my one-sided affair with Roland,
she remarked that she had hoped to never meet me.

"I told her I had an ineluctable impulse to come —
to meet and evaluate Roland's choice —
and that between us she was the better choice.
I lied of course — since I will always be
the one that Roland should have picked."

WELSHING

He brought out the suicide pact from his briefcase
and motioned, "Sign it." "I love you Ransford,"
I assured him, "but not that much."

In my dream I was standing on the edge
of a five-mile-deep pit, contemplating
nonexistence.

"You did exactly right not to sign."
"I had agreed, you know, previously."
"Nevertheless you were quite within your rights."

I placed an imaginary gun
against my real left eyebrow
and pulled an imaginary trigger.
Then I told Ransford to go ahead without me.

PART III
The Metaphysical

DEATH IN DREAMS

(The Interpretation of Nightmares)

To Eileen Squires

Ostinato

It started, Dr. Erikson, as an experience of epiphany
with an uneven kettledrumming in my ear on D and E
whose blurred pattern I hoped to catch
by cupping and tuning my ears.

Now the entry of a xylophone
in scales of open fifths,
a harpsichordist trilling with both hands,
a syncopation in the horn on A and D —

the musicians were arranged in a semicircle.
The accompaniment was prepared
for the entrance of a solo voice.
Who was to be the soloist?

I seemed to be receiving, yet was unequipped to take,
musical dictation, without a notebook of staff paper,
without pen or source of light. The stars were in.
Was it known that I was not the soloist
and had never learned or heard the solo part?

In early morning still, still intensely dark,
I saw in a corner field of my eye
the conductor in tails, staring badly —
god-like or half or wholly mad —

who beat the time by wrapping and unwrapping his arms
as if willing to tear them off
if the music asked it of him

to separate into even parts
these units of moments
out of all inordinate time.

I tried to fix each instrument's notes
in a safe and protected spot of the mind
for future transcription to manuscript
in case this god-sent inspiration, my first,

was a significant addition to the world's canon.
(Regrettably, the solo part was missing.)
It started as a kettledrumming inside my ear
as Karl Maria von Weber might have heard in his.

Call to Action

In this poor light,
beyond the musicians in the pit,
I spotted another figure in a Buddha pose,
seated in front of the flaps of a tent
in a posture of inner research,
legs and arms neatly folded and stored,
so enviably serene.

Of what persuasion, faith, or lodge
I was uncertain. Was he a Hermann Hesse,
a shaman, prophet, or psychopomp,
the ensi Gudea of Lagash,
or a religious order of his own?

His hair arranged formally in rows of snails,
wearing a short skirt of furry pelts
(in which First Kingdom Sumerians
customarily posed for their statuary),
he reworked his *Code of Totality Symbols*
with a stylus.

With him I felt in the presence of my intercessor
who had access to God's ear (alchemic and all-hearing)
and determinations (wholly correct); he would drag me
before Him if I lost my taste for a closing defense:

that I had done my utmost and was willing
to do what I should — if I had known what it was.
One must keep in mind the autonomous unconscious
I was given to outwit — and the fragmentary will.

I renounced my formal faith the day of birth.
While left illimitably free, and free of gods and trappings,
I am left unloved by any mythic being.

Can you picture this tent, Dr. Erikson?
Exactly, exactly the one of Piero della Francesca's
Dream of Constantine in the Arezzo Chapel.
The tent of my nightmare was the one of Piero's vision
of Constantine's dream.

An art historian by training,
I tend to see my surroundings
as like or unlike the works of art I know.
I hope to be thought of as a gentleman and scholar,
but one never knows how one is regarded by others.

Sign

The Buddha in sheepskin posted a sign on his tent:
"Enter herein
to experience the private visions of the visionaries,
relive the ecstasies of Saints Teresa and Eustacia,
imitate the imitations of Thomas à Kempis;
private instruction from Luther, Calvin, Wesley, Eddy.
Hear the faith defended by that subtlest of thinkers,
Aquinas. Others from a wide choice of beliefs.
Eastern to the left. Western to the right.
Healers, soothers, unclassified believers —
straight ahead."

This might be an underworld night-sea journey
in the tradition of Buddha, Virgil, Dante, Auden,
I cautioned myself. Refuse, refuse.
Be wary. Remember how
your fears will reoccur.
I read further:

"Second Act. An irreplaceable experience.
A scene from the film, *Lives of Composers,*
photographed in the reassembled past from life,
utilizing light waves formerly dispersed in space
by secret processes of almost unfeasible technology.

"That is, specifically witness:
G. P. Telemann and J. S. Bach compete on the organ
for the Leipzig position of Kapellmeister.
See poor Bach lose and shake both hands of G. P. Telemann.
The loser will play a Toccata in B Minor (since lost),
and freely improvise on the notes D, E, A, and D.

The irony of the sublime Bach rejected
should give undying hope to any loser.

"Refreshments. All invited. Free.
Now enter the tent at once."

I was tempted and thought it worth
whatever loss of time or psychic damage
it required.
A musicologist by avocation,
I am writing a "Life and Works,"
among other efforts, of Telemann
and intend to prove the Leipzig position
was injurious to his artistry —
that worldly success numbs one.

Hesitation

Upon this firm decision to enter, I was beset by
unclear memories of Harry Haller's door in the wall.
As far as I understand myself,
I am fearful by nature, particularly of *change*.
I am troubled at births and dissolve at deaths.
An embarkation, even to a pleasure spot
such as Watteau's Cythera, causes me
days of discomfort beforehand —
a tight constriction in my heart and throat —
as I gather specks of courage one by one.

As a fixed rule, I prefer the known
and regularly refuse all calls to adventure.
I hope to slip unnoticed past all risks.
And die thereby — fearlessly in bed.

Did I tell you, Doctor, the tent was in royal, royalest blue
with gold swags and tassels, with pendulating tassels?
Four minarets at each corner of the circular tent
against a black field with many white moons.
Can you compose this scene in your mind
with the colors I saw,
the royal blue, white, black, and gold?
I could not not go in.

Theater

I entered the tent (unnerving my conscious,
my Jungian shadow took over)
into a private theater, a *tempietto*,
a miniature hall with a single seat.
Where were the other seats?
I was too absorbed by a Tiepolo ceiling
to account for this removal from logic.

How did Tiepolo
find this inner shell of an Easter egg
to decorate?
How did the theater's owner find Tiepolo?
A king's mistress might stage theatricals here
if kings had mistresses these kingless days.

The decoration of domes and ceilings
is not an interest of our times;
nor is building oneself a Medici tomb
with exhausted nudes to adorn one's ashes.
So many ceilings are now unpainted,
and tomb design — my special interest —
is an obsolescent art.

Marble palm trees replaced ionic columns
in the aisles. Next to my seat I noted
a Maillol sculpture of a standing nude
in bronze, radiating energy, implying powers of action.

A gentleman in a bowler hat, fully clothed,
by Nadelman, in wood, was waiting in a niche
with face to wall, owing to personal embarrassments.

Other than I , and the sculptures,
no one was present;
but the theater was full —
you remember it only seated one.

The lights were abruptly cut.
Miss Maillol took my hand
or I took hers. Yes, I admit
I took hers for comfort —
her wet, hot bronze hand, straight from a foundry.

The curtains were pulled open with short wrenches.
The same musicians were in the pit
performing the theme for kettledrum
that I was to compose upon waking.

A film screen was lowered. A cinema.
A favorite form of mine for self-indulgence,
for trying the experiences of others
more venturesome than I while risking nothing.

I stared at the waves scattering in water sprays
and water banners, at a spine of water arching upwards —
more precisely, an upward flowing waterfall —
and at showers of water veils descending.

The waves exploded, bloomed, broke up, and dropped —
limp and timid at our feet.
The efflorescence was too brief
to formulate an apt comparison:

I thought of the bronze of *Zeus*
Hurling the Thunderbolt, a favorite of mine,
(Athens, National Museum, circa 460 B.C.) —
his arms pulling apart in opposite directions.

Vision

Each wave lasted a flick, a blink —
the speed of thought —
and tore itself apart.

I was arrested by the sight of, the trajectory of,
waves; my hypnotizer was the water spouts.
I sensed — I admit it smelled of —
the setting for a vision in a Hofmannthal film.
Would I mind a vision if I must have one?

The hope of a revealed system, of any belief
to which I could subscribe wholeheartedly —
sent by a private message or a visitation,
seen in a bush, wave, dream, burning babe,
by any sign, stigmata, Inanna on her ziggurat —
was a harmless hope of mine since I had given up
my formal religion as a child.

Thus I was predisposed to accept a revelation
in the hurtling sheets of water jets —
to read the transparent words on the water beads.

Now three-story waves came to my attention,
each wave lunging higher than the next.
Is my beatific vision changed to threats?
Did I read the complex water symbol incorrectly?
Was it a renewal, a higher elevation, a further growth —
or was it a dissolution, a drowning,
the end of me and all my trying?

My vision was as follows:
in the prismatic droplets of water spray
I recognized the galaxies and celestial bodies
of our universe. And I, privileged —
abandoning the inconvenience of body,
now pure mind — was standing beyond the cosmos,
vaulted beyond physical space, looking in.

Conversing with and thanking the Prime Mover,
with gentleness and tact, I declined
the handsome offer
of immortal life or continual rebirth.
I tried not to hurt Him, but He *was* affected.

I was called back to myself,
to consciousness within the dream —
to the beach with Maxwell posing Miss Maillol —
by my feet awash inside my shoes.

Death

It was a winter's day at the beach.
I am sure it was sun in winter
rather than snow in summer.
Maxwell's cameras were mounted on tripods in the snow
facing the waves of the day — an uninviting icy blue —
each wave five stories high or higher.

I remarked to the actress next to me, Miss Maillol,
"These waves must set records —
for heights of waves in winter,"
who spread a blanket over the snow and prepared to sun
without a comment. Suffering from her snub,
I tried to maintain my liking for myself.

She removed her coat of lynx, her smock of silk,
her tutu, and sunned in a flesh-colored suit
that would appear as skin in the film.

Each wave was driving in and vaulting up
before collapsing at our feet.
Although the others were untroubled,
we all seemed in danger of washing away.
Hugging my arms around my knees,
I knew my face revealed much fear.

"The waves will never reach us:
I know waves." Miss Maillol winked
and patted my nose and buttoned my coat.
I felt warm gratitude for her acceptance
of the weakness I could never overcome.

The waves moved higher, swiping overhead,
the rope trick of a Trickster in a swarming figure eight,
but gaining power, moment, portent —
each one licking closer to our feet.

I bent to Miss Maillol to advise us to retreat,
but she was sunning on her back, content, smiling
to herself. I preferred not to disturb her.
Rather than announce my fear, I now preferred to drown.

The crew was even closer to the undertow, wading in foam.
Trying to film the droplets of spray,
Maxwell was under the lip of a wave —
bobbing under now, now wholly submerged.
Nadelman was floating face down —
the end of his embarrassments.

Reprieve

An awesome wave, twice higher than the rest,
ten stories high, whipped in overhead,
stretching upward, ripping water.
To my student of beauty's eye,
a sight worth dying young for.

I noticed, with dread, this innocuous water spray
transformed in mid-air
into a mass of threatening snow —
into an avalanche of snow
suspended over our heads —
about to pound down upon us, embed us in snow,
freeze us, smother us — to my utmost shock.

We will never survive the present moment,
the moment I have always feared.
A mold of snow will pour tight around us,
and we, the sacrificed originals,
will be found later frozen *in situ*.

I tried to reach the actress
for a hug before the end,
at least to die with a friend and fellow victim,
before the mass of falling snow sealed us over.

The terror of realization:
in a split second the end
of me, the start of oblivion.
The beginning of the endless.
And I without any help here or hereafter.
O god, this smothering of snow.
We both died before I reached her.

Now, Doctor, do you think my subterranean mind
had planned all along to intimidate me,
to induce this state of extreme dread,
beguiling me into the theater and other ploys:
the Nadelman, the Maillol, the Tiepolo.
Using my weaknesses to tempt me forward.

If so, I disown it. I disown my own mind.
I still can see the airborne mass of snow —
swaying, threatening, stalking overhead —
to pour down upon me and the undeserving Maillol.

I will never understand how I can wish
to scare myself, to punish myself, so excessively.
While assuming oneself safely in bed,

one's mind induces a state so like death
that one believes one has indeed smothered to death.
On waking, one must adjust to being still alive:
my physical heart, constricted in pain, recovers slowly.
One could, in fact, easily *die*
from the fearful effects of such a nightmare.

HIBISCUS

1.

O sweet one in the hibiscus bush,
step down and worship me.
Give up your former gods, pursuit of the good,
and safe passage on the way.
Unfold your altar rug and worship me.
You will be all the faithful I require.

One god is equal to another
the anthropologists submit:
one need not apologize for an eccentric faith.
I recommend acceptance of mortality,
a compromise of body and spirit,
and other tenets I will later promulgate.

Then, sweet one, forget the worn-out faiths:
the monasteries no longer lead the way,
the mystics are confused by all that now is known,
the cosmologists, thwarted taking measurements
by the unthinkable emptiness of space,
search for satisfying numerical descriptions
and avoid the dilemmas of existence.

A dying god is washing toward your feet
brought by a swell to the edge of your toes
on the last wave before the ocean
leaves its ocean bed and streams into space.

2.

One sees the many Jews out touring
in their Mercedes Benz grand touring cars
as a gracious and forgiving group.
Has it been thirty years, do you recall,
since all that decimation?

Or should one not maintain a lasting grudge?
When is the seemly time to abandon regrets for
dead members of our human race, fellow members
of our civilization that crumpled down once more.
How many times will our mutual race forget itself
and be able to proceed with any confidence?

That the faith still obtains
after this unsettling decimation —
too unspeakable and gross
to consider in an ordered way —
is a tribute to man's faith in testing,
large-scale testing to the edges of collapse.

One must produce a faith beyond all meaning
to withstand these maulings of the wits.
I cannot easily adapt to this scar, a scar
not easily expunged from the record of our human race.

It is in general the murderer's fault,
but in time one finds the sorting of evidence futile,
even blaming the victims for not outwitting bullets,
and leaving us this worry of injustice done.
Since nothing can compensate the dead for their deaths,
we suggest a general pardon for all the irresponsible.

The chosen, so-called by themselves, were simply forsaken.
The Mercedes is a pleasant car for peacetime touring.

3.

The radioactive bombing of the Japanese — other members
of our mutual race — needs further clarification.
Harry Truman and others and I thought the mission
a clever expedient: less of us dead than of them —
in the attitude of one's time. One does embrace
the attitude of one's time: their deserving it.

4.

One can withdraw one's faith in deities,
but may one resign from the human race?
While alive, one cannot not participate in being.
Whatever the race plans to do without my consent,
I now withdraw my membership before it is done:
I am no longer responsible for my contemporaries'
conduct of the human race.

5.

Since I myself hold long-lived grudges,
I am still holding a detailed grudge in behalf of
my dead great-uncle, swindled from his pittance.
Perhaps my uncle was misinformed of his rightful share;
perhaps a submissive uncle deserves to be snatched
from his pittance — for insufficient self-assertion.

I myself believe in long-term grudges
until Marvell's conversion of the Jews,
who want no newer faith (however inappropriate
to decimation) than that which helped
their tribal fathers escape the Pharaoh,
himself seeking other visions of immortal being.
More human dissatisfaction with mortality.

6.

Nietzsche is much maligned:
his sister and others recast his thought, edited
his texts, papers, notes — to mean other than he meant —
after all his efforts at precise expression.
Nietzsche only found out what he meant
by studying his own self-imposed destruction.
Who holds the grudge for enemies of Nietzsche's thought?

It is not too bad a fate to be my enemy.
All my enemies do well and continue to do well.

7.

Then, sweet one, abandon the hibiscus;
the universe is ours, if viewed with disengagement.
Let us observe the untrammeled stars, pure motion,
the edges of space, the remote novae,
the even more remote supernovae,
and abandon the race to its own headlong undoing.

Leaving your former gods to their well-known indifference,
we will invent new and uncompromised replacements.
Therefore, sweet one, come to your new-found deity —
although I despise all those who grasp the power.

PART IV
Temptations

THE IMMORALITY OF DREAMS

This was becoming one of my finest dreams
I remember telling myself as it unfolded.

Coming toward me, she was wearing a white and yellow
thin transparent loose curtain or blouse
and long loose drapery with floating swags,

and a purple skirt and purple stockings.
On her dazzling agile feet she wore heavy platform shoes
that made much noise as she took steps.

I knew her name was Vivian from a prior dream.

My wife was peering out behind a narrow
two-story Venetian blind with one thousand slats,

but I preferred not to notice her poor taste —
without any evidence of my wrongdoing up to this dream.

If I had time in the dream and I hadn't already told her,
I intended to regale Vivian with my long oboe solo
missed — the exposed oboe cadenza in Beethoven's wearisome
Fifth — how I locked myself into a nearby room
to warm my lip and never heard the concert start.

As I attempted to slip Vivian past my residence,
I wished she would lift her heavy shoes with greater care
and make less clatter.

The sidewalk before my house kept stretching forward
as if pulled by some unknown elastic forces.
It took us, I would say, two hours to pass the far window.

My wife's cat kept running underfoot and tripping Vivian.
Of the many good routes I knew, why had I chosen
this hazardous route in full view of my wife and her ally?

Boldly guiding and pulling Vivian along, I thought
how unlike me to display so much assurance.
Understand that I had to make these lascivious advances;
I was given no moral choices in the dream,

no matter what the price — expulsion, endless abuse, no peace —
no matter what my wife threatened,
even if she brought up for review
our eternal pact of faithfulness.

Despite the evidence of meanness to which she admitted,
I had remained close to her — due to inertia —
and overlooked many of her overt faults.

Vivian was tiring and stopped to fix her shoe strap.

Eventually I found a marble stairwell that seemed free
in a house we had occupied when I was four,
with a copy of Correggio's *Io* still in its frame —
Zeus in the form of a small cloud
causing Io to shudder.

At the prospect of the immediate present,
I could feel my smile stream forth excessively;
the edges of my mouth were strained from all my smiling.

Did I look too pleased or inexperienced?
As a general rule, I have always tried
to look experienced
no matter how inexperienced I am.

Her hand was insufferably comforting.
The pain of the pleasure of touching this hand,
her source of feeling, unhinged me.

I felt a victim of mystic and other more radical sensations:
primordial instinctual
acute desire.

I was planning next to lift my left hand
to her shoulder in one suave connected motion,
with a speed that she could not deflect,

to pin her shoulders to the wall
and move my face on a left diagonal plane
toward her receptive lips.

As the modulation approached the new tonality,

either my wife rearranging the pillows at her neck
and elbows, or my deception in the act of dreaming
(in which I broke the faithful record of ten years),
or a burst of cosmic light on my latent worries,

one of these causes woke me to the double deprivation
of losing my incomplete dream

to bare stale pallid actuality —
and of losing my perfect, if bodiless, Vivian
to my wife, who is somewhat better company than no one.

After describing to my wife
how I was cheated of the blissful conclusion
to my outing with Vivian,

she interpreted and completed my dream:
"Before you had a chance to further
your prurient schemes with Vivian, her brother

found and beat you mildly as a warning —
and sent you back to me.
I took you in begrudgingly.
We still have each other."

I explained to my wife, who was
very pleased with her dream analysis,
that I consider myself entirely faithful.

But am I entirely faithful
if I am happily unfaithful
in many of my major dreams?

WITH EUGENE IN THE CAR

Seated comfortably in the palace
of his green car, I spread my skirt in a semicircle
over my legs and the seat on both sides.

My skin felt newly bathed and powdered:
I felt the powder specks rest on my bare arms.

To be enclosed with Eugene in his speeding car
was all that I ever hoped for —
that particular night of my life.

I was quiet and attentive at first
as he talked of his own
and the world's malaise,

but soon my mind was planning
what I might say later in the evening,
what I might allow later in the evening,

when all is less strained, less formal,
when the powder flecks have drifted off my arms.

I had recently abandoned —
as my preferred attitude —
loving-kindness toward all

and now assess individuals
separately, as they prove themselves to be.

In addition, after much introspection,
I now wish to release myself
from persistent attempts at goodness.

Goodness, with all its restrictions,
limits one's ability to experience widely.
However, after falling into serious difficulties,
I intend to work my way back —
and reform completely.

Slowly rolling up the window,
I close out everyone
who populates this road.

Except for another,
one needs no one on such occasions.
Our private car is all the world we want.

If I'm planning — as I am —
to allow Eugene to seduce me,
it will not be a true seduction,
since I am not initially reluctant.

The role thrust upon me by my family's
religiosity — my father as a member of the clergy,
my close relationship to the Way — understandably
puts constraints on the mood of my escorts.

My personal convictions are tentative:
the omnipotent by definition
knows we err and somehow acquiesces.

If one posits an omnipotent godhead,
free will seems improbable — in any logical system.
Without free will, one is a tool;
with it, one's god is semipotent.

The faith says we may forego logic
as long as we believe wholeheartedly;
I am leaving unresolved matters of belief
until I have time to reflect further

but suspect neither faith nor logic
nor any of the religions can save me
from the temptations to which I plan to succumb.

I am blessed with strong shoulders
and a sturdy body that works well;
I am described as having a passive, bland expression

that does not accurately reflect
my intensity, my inner swarming state.

Eugene, drive me to a spot I've never been before,
sheltered from disquieting thoughts
and intruders stumbling upon us.
Protect our pleasure from all distractions.

I leaned against the fur-lined seat
of the palace car, experiencing perfect comfort.

Eugene stopped the car at the edge
of a sharply plunging cliff.
Pushing his head backwards on the seat,

his profile facing the low car roof, he appeared
stricken by some disheartening recollection.

Perhaps he wished he were with
someone more entertaining.

Suggesting that we return, he started the engine.
I was despondent at the prospect:
that nothing works out
is my experience of this life.

He drove on a few feet and stopped
the car abruptly in a field of tall grass.

Without warning, he suddenly
burrowed his curly, wiry hair
under my blouse. I tentatively kissed
his curls; my temptation was under way.

After several minutes, he abruptly stopped
printing my body with satisfying kisses.
"We shouldn't be doing this," he whispered hoarsely.
"You're right, of course, to think of that."
I could not admit
that I was seducible.

I spread my skirt out in a semicircle
and no longer felt the powder flecks
resting on my arms.

Moving away from a position of goodness
is not as easily accomplished as I would have thought.

UNDER ONE OF THE GEORGES

We were lying on a black rug of damp grass
offering ourselves up to the warm night breezes
in a formal park with geometric paths and plantings
and stretches of flat and even grass near Queen's Way.

Having chosen a spot beneath a statue of George One or Three,
we were alternately drinking undiluted gin and kissing lightly,
and regretting that George One or Three was dead
and would therefore miss our drinking party
and the evening's sumptuous breezes.
"Long live all dead kings!" Trevor shouted, quite unlike him.

Trevor, my delight, recently revising his personality,
now spoke in an affected manner, which he hoped might suit:
"A first-class breeze is a treat of the tactile senses,
the manna of hedonists. I am a devotee of the breeze
and when one becomes available I drop all obligations,

rush out, take rough measurements in the field
of temperature and pressure, evaluate my findings,
and compare these with earlier samples in my breeze collection,
which exists only in the memory of the researcher.
No one can preserve a breeze in motion, its pouring
around one's skin —." At the zenith of our revels,

a jarring intrusion — a sinusoidal wave of sound.
Beyond our sight, beyond the flat, black grass,
the disembodied voice of an unknown reformer,
a self-appointed judge of the occasion and
one with little sense of the rarity of perfect pleasure,

called — bellowed — across the stretch of low black lawn:
"One is not allowed to procreate on the Queen's own Way.
Take yourselves home for such activity.
Poor examples of the British subject."
I, less sensitive to world opinion, reassured
and patted Trevor, who realigned his jacket and tie.

I could sense that Trevor was downcast by the aspersion
on his taste. His light heart, his hilarity had fled.
"I myself don't mind," I said. "Let whoever wishes to believe
in his own mistaken views feel free to do so. I feel
it isn't worth the effort of the almost innocent
to protest any calumny. Do you agree or not?"

And Trevor, my delight, with his highly developed sense
of fitness and all his appropriate manners and tact,
who never did more than take my arm and rotate it
admiringly and contemplate its form in the round,
was troubled.

Often flattering me excessively, he would rhapsodize:
"The shape of your arm, its articulation,
function, and structure, strikes me as unmatched
in the entire documented history of the arm.
I have never found an arm — even Phidias himself never found
    an arm
from which to model the lost *Pallas Athena* — as fine as yours
in its ability to distract a viewer from cares."

Only recently had Trevor placed his body near my body
discreetly, so that we might transfer heat flow and ions;
just last night, Trevor had learned to kiss my forehead —
while continuing to lie very close and study the form of my arm.
But always with the compunctions of the celibate weakening.

I hoped our unknown voice of the night felt comforted —
now that he had destroyed our temptations, annihilated
our perfect pleasures, and dispersed a rare collector's breeze;
the improvement of others is the aspiration of the confident:
I myself would never wish to make improvements in others,
not that confident of my grasp of the correct direction.

Where I was leading Trevor, down or up, depends wholly
on one's perspective on the landscape, and I prefer the view
at night when nothing is distinct. I know it is poor form
to defend oneself at too much length; however, as I recall
from my Chaucer, if it weren't for procreation,
where would we all be?

In keeping with my nature, I accept the full guilt of crimes
as accused, both those I did and did not commit.

A BIRD WATCH

An obese jay took his perch on a branch
near my porch. His feathers barely covered his girth.
I had never, being city-born, seen before an obese jay,
who overate whatever it is jays eat.
Despite his breadth, he could still cruise smoothly
between the ladders of pine branches —
just as certain plump men dance suavely —
preening for, I saw her, another obese jay.
He pursued her between the grid of branches,
finally caught and gave her a forceful hug.
Nothing yet too passionate to watch.
He next exhibited his skills in flying —
a dive into a spin into an oval orbit —
a blatant self-display that I frown on in myself.
She joined him and they flew a formation,
wing tips touching, dipping in and out of currents.
I sensed he adored her. He rifled her feathers.
Was I a bird watcher or a voyeur? I shut my eyes.

PART V

Compensations

THE ENTHUSIAST

Quick, find me a brush —
the colors black, white, and pink
a small paper and a water jar
and hope I can paint
from memory
the fleeting sight
and spirit of her:

A lady in a doorway of black hair
this hair a spillway, a waterfall, a storm cloud
the doorway resting on black beds of fox fur collar
the face embedded in a black oval setting of feathers
a white face powdered even whiter with dust of alabaster
and double peaks of lips
colored pink

whom I saw driving in her car
and could have loved, given any chance,
if she had stopped
when I threw myself
under her wheels.

NIGHTLIFE

The cat jumped on the dog who dropped
from the bed and I woke up to the harp
of breaking glass.

That I couldn't see the scrub pines
confirmed the clock, settled on three
and never open to discussion.

Four hours to sleep — much needed sleep —
before I could begin my work day
in which I lose contact with myself
in the endless details I attend to
and in some cases do not attend to.

Forty miles from here by train,
on the twenty-fourth floor by elevator,
silent and mechanically dependable,
is my Office of Details.

The woods more patiently
than the pets wait for me
to return each evening,
at which time I run
through the brush to keep fit.
And to restore lost contact with myself.

I sensed that I had no intention
of being put back to bed
to lie awake for hours
reviewing unpleasant incidents,
my usual custom on these occasions —

although I needed my sleep
more desperately than usual
to make up for recent omissions
and to oversee my details properly.

I stumbled out to the car
to find my three-tiered tool chest
with its drawing equipment ready
for last night's night class I had missed
after an unpleasant incident
brought on by my omitting a necessary detail.

I propped my block of paper against
a three-legged chair; the fourth was chewed
off by the dog protesting my absence
at drawing class, risking my displeasure
in a desperate show of love.

I wish any one of my friends
could love me that completely.

I surveyed the cabin
for what might be appropriate to draw.
Catching sight of an unclear image
in a frame, with untrimmed beard,
erratic eyebrows, and a dazed stare,
I recognized myself looking
particularly unfit.

A drawing of discovery:
a triangle established my arm,
a black rain established my mind;
a connecting vector joined my hand
to my mind.

After an hour's thought, I added
a transition from mind to submind
with a series of light gray spirals,
narrowing to represent opaque unconscious.

After one hour more, I added a grid
in the right upper quadrant
to represent my sense of prison
and recognition that these releases
would be only temporary —
moments amidst years.

I then faced this confusing realization:
that I might contact myself only
accidentally, when not looking,
and might miss myself in passing
or when sleeping.

At seven o'clock, now time to dress, now light,
the enthusiasm for my drawing crested —
I couldn't recall, within my lifetime,
one unpleasant incident
that had ever happened to me.

Dressed in my heavy winter jacket and boots,
I rested for fifteen minutes across my bed
before setting out toward the details
to lose myself for hours,
still looking particularly unfit.
By now I was tired, very tired.

THE REGULATED SIDE OF SELF
ADDRESSES THE UNREGULATED

"You are getting nowhere," I warned myself.
"Write it down in your journal:
that you have not made progress
much beyond breakfast this morning,
still sitting with your cup, your two cups,
of cool brown water — utterly unable to move."

One must learn diversionary techniques
to accomplish what needs to be done,
to turn the routine into a more remarkable activity
overriding the anfractuous mind and its unwilling body
and the philistine tribes that surround one.

"The soothing water bath awaits you, Louis, rise.
Don't concern yourself just now with royal duties,
those arduous tasks of governing.
Think only of submerging yourself in the pools
of Versailles, with spouting fountains as companions,
terracotta bathing ladies, and courtiers to hold
your robes and thoroughly scrub your back."

"I cannot attend my morning levee;
tell our fellow nobles. I don't wish
to play today at divine-right kings.
Besides, Louis had assistance at his levees.
I need someone to assist with my dressing,

to find my daily working robes, the wig, the garters.
I'll rest here while fresh clothing is embroidered with suns.
Was Louis perturbed that the sun was its own master?"

"Confess the cause of tiredness to the good reader:
too much bragging, truth-seeking, drinking,
explaining self to others who do not wish to hear.
Too much Mozart, Dohnanyi, Dvorak.
You should have put your instrument away at eleven.
Look at what it has done to you — a pitiful clump.
More self-regulation is in order.
Moderate your pleasure seeking in proportion to — ."

"Friend of mine, with my significant interests at heart,
when I am ready for the day to start —
probably tomorrow — I will send a message.
Right now, I am looking for the Montespan.
As for bathing, it was said of Louis
by a mistress who should know
'qu'il puait comme une charogne' —
that he stank like a carcass."

THE WHITE TOWER
(A Novel in the Form of a Poem)

We went to the movies and saw nothing.
Instead we made plans to marry on Friday,
both sixteen and wanting each other.
He would work as a cook and I as a waitress
at the White Tower if we lied about our age.

We would either rent the garage of a boarded mansion
(and wash in the Esso Station) or the main house with ballroom,
for sale for thirty years and not yet sold,
whose porch cantilevered over the harbor
in which we dove for soft-souled crabs
until Geoffrey dislocated his neck on a rock.

He now watches our dives from his motorized wheelchair
with an iron bar to tie his arms to his back.
"At least avoid mistakes you know about,"
was father's comment on Geoffrey's condition.
Should we elope or have a church service

on the rocks with Geoffrey reading Psalm 8:
"When I look up to the heaven, the work of thy fingers,
The moon and the stars that thou hast made:
What is man that thou shouldst think of him?"
(I for one do not believe — my study of archaeology,
researches on early man's theology and comparative religions

seem to have rendered the Testaments mythical for me —
the word of man.

However, I admire your little human's attempts,
with short-lived mortality unacceptable,
to try to will himself significant in the scheme,
not stranded and tucked off in the stars, unneeded;
to make this point, earlier poets would call on the moth,
ephemeral fleas, or the day lily; but nature seems to me outlived.)

What about cooking? We would eat all meals
at the White Tower and lie about our inexperience
and age. Expedient lying might be acceptable
if one hurts no one, *"neminem laede,"*
although I cannot prove it. Nor could Schopenhauer
in *Die beiden Grundprobleme der Ethik.*
I read widely, for my questions, in those
who think — or thought — for a living.

The marriage lasted a weekend. From Friday to Monday.
We were wholly unsuited: his trombone and other mannerisms.
I married again at eighteen. This second persisted
longer. My second husband, after a year, fell
or jumped out a window from a fifth-floor bathtub —
naked — and lived five minutes. The policeman,
new to the profession, was sick on himself and of no use.

Our neighbor, Mr. Oxburg, was dining at the window
of his cellar apartment when he saw the body splat.
He couldn't decide to finish his peas or not,
or rush out to help and be accused of curiosity,
or stay hidden in bed from this cleft of hell.
In any case, he canceled his custard.

"Why did you? Why didn't you let me explain?"
I screamed at him dead or dying. "Some of the time,
when asked, I was faithful. At least half the time."
That he had failed his first year engineering
turned out to be a contributing cause
that cut my share of the blame in half.
Unknown to me, he was faithful and unknown to him, I was not.
In spirit, if not body, I felt myself true in every respect.

It was, God knows, embarrassing that he killed himself
in the courtyard. Open season for innuendoes.
I felt I wore a phosphorescent scarlet letter
and called the baby Pearl. Why not?
I resolved not to marry for at least ten years.

Rufus was a medical intern with the reddish hair I like.
(Disassociated from the White Tower,
I now worked at a Kidney Clinic in charge of
emergency removal of spilled blood or vomit.)
I thought of myself as a Mary Magdalene
doing a sentence of penance; it helps me to improve
plain states of living by imaginary feats. (My third
husband, Hooker, dead of a kidney transplant at 22.)

Although red-haired Rufus liked me well enough,
by his analyses I was not of his intellectual strata:
he wanted a wife with a master's degree or publications.
I did not explain I took the Great Books Course off and on
and persisted with it. Self-taught, I hoped to become —
by practicing a Socratic method of questioning all —
a foremost living humanist and clearly would, in time,
move away from Rufus and his closed system.
I mean, from all the extended chaos and miasma I am in,
to acquire, in a private search for purpose,
the teleological point of one's existence.

I am tiring of the type of man I like and pick;
Errol, a music teacher, with a nervous tic rhythmically
hopping his cheek, didn't care for Pearl.
I have faults, both evident and hidden,
but I would never send tentative Pearl away
although aware I don't like her as much as I should —
she reminds me of her father's face lying in blood.

Well, I suppose I am meant to survive the future —
I now have all the finest thoughts arranged in mind
but matching them to action in the enfilade eludes me.
I have recently met Wallace just released from jail,
(embezzlement of a Christmas Club Fund, never proved)
who likes Pearl. It might work out.
If it doesn't, one still has one's better thoughts.

Although my experience suggests I should not be,
I am stubbornly hopeful.
When the group leader at the clinic announced
he was to spring bad news, I thought with an inside smile
only the worst can touch me —
I was to be replaced by an automatic cleaning unit.
In a sense, I am above disaster.

NOTES TO HIMSELF
FOR PREPARING HIS CONFESSION

By Henry Schmidt, Positivist

Excerpt 15 March 1950

I am wrestling with my sadness today.
We struggle back and forth.
Sadness is swamping me;
the arm of sadness is raised.

A review of the past
always with terror
at what I said and felt —
how could I have
held such transient notions?

My skin is alligatory;
my eyelids twitch.
I see as well as ever
but seeing is deceptive.

I always have had the finest set of eyes
for looking at specks — 20/20 vision.
I wish I had had perfect pitch
to accompany my eyes
and a capacious memory.

Perhaps my ideas are still deceptions,
not true ideas. When will I know

I have approached closest to the truth?
I am studying the Positivists.

I am not one to surrender to believing
or waive my powers of reason
as so many before me leaping to their faith.
Even my friend Eliot deserted uncertainty.

While I am longing for capacities,
I would request a singing voice
to move the souls of nonbelievers
and opera lovers, and any others who need fervor.

A voice to express the range of pain and beauty,
to drive the note to its full meaning,
gaining revelation and momentum —
and letting go.

I took my own poor advice:
no one is to blame although
I would like to blame anyone
willing to accept it.

I didn't think deeply or completely:
it was my own quality of mind
that lacked rigor
to choose between the truths available.

The Positivists disallow metaphysics
and what cannot be verified by the senses:
the various types of gods are useless
and no one knows the good from the better or worse.
I am temporarily a Positivist.